slopjar

Ingrid Jennings

SlopJar

By:Ingrid Jennings

SlopJar

ISBN: 978-0-9856960-4-7

Library of Congress Control Number: 2012910128

Lioness Publishing House

P.O. Box 223204

West Palm Beach, FL 33422

Dedication

This book is dedicated to the dreadful people in my life that have inspired me to creativity and have shaped my life into SlopJar. I also dedicate this book to my darling granddad who inspired me to be the best at whatever I do, my mother who shaped my personality, my sisters and brothers whom I love so dearly, my husband (what am I without you?), my son who brings laughter to my life, and the most wonderful being in the universe, GOD.

Table of Contents

❧ LAUGHTER

Prelude

Get ready to indulge in the mind of a paranoid schizophrenic woman whose delusions cause her to do an unspeakable act. She then gets locked up in a mental institution, where she begins to write.

lunatic

NIGHTMARES

Too many nightmares live in my mind,

too many nightmares leave me in a bind,

too many nightmares surround my soul,

they leave me in fear,

when no one is near.

Too many nightmares,

oh, why are you here?

Leave me in peace

so I may sleep.

And here I go

down to dream.

Sleep be sweet and lay me in rest.

CANDLELIGHT

And as I lay down to sleep,

I felt that dream that burdens my soul,

so softly it tiptoed in,

I could see its apparition whisk by my body

-in my long-lost dream.

The dream once lost came back to haunt.

For days I never knew what peace was like.

So here I slumber,

I slumber in light

because I'm scared with fright

of this mysterious ghost haunting my dreams.

Dreams of flowers,

dreams of bliss,

dreams of this thing

coming out at night.

So I slumber in light.

The light of a candle burning on my chest,

please put me to rest

and rid me of this pest.

And here I slumber,

in the light of the fire,

undisturbed by all spirits' desires.

And the apparition of smoke so softly whisks

    by my bed,

the flames of the candle dance in its presence.

I have been frightened, so I burn my candle at night.

And my candle burns each night and blazes so high.

And me—

I lie,

seeking a restful night,

undisturbed by any little fright.

Until I awaken in a hospital bed,

Thank God for men of fire.

They came in the night and rescued my soul,

they saved my flesh from the flames of the night.

THE DREAM

It has already been determined how much

    I burned my candle because of a

haunting in a dream.

A dream so extreme,

it felt so supreme,

call it blasphemy,

because this dream made me scream.

A dream where I dreamt of cedar and oak

    romancing my figure and caressing my body

    under a starry sky.

A sky so intensifying,

it bewildered my mind.

Under the starry sky

I didn't feel any lack,

any lack of love,

for I knew it was all there.

And in this dream the woods

capture my soul.

The cedar and oak entangle me so.

Why do they do so,

seduce me each night?

They entangle me in their bewildering webs.

I just float through the night

in the midst of the shadows.

I dance with the branches,

I play with the leaves

until the dawn begins to rise.

And just as it rises,

it sets just as well,

and when it does my friends and I

begin to dance.

In a trance

we move about.

The glowing moon watches from above.

We twirl and we run.

We enjoy the sounds of a sleepless night.

Why do these woods entangle me so,

wrapping me in their bewildering webs?

When the fall comes they shelter my body

from cold frost bites, and as the winter tiptoes in

I run about,

there's no doubt.

Trotting on the leaves,

scouting through the forest.

Pecan, cedar, oak, or maple,

I love my trees.

They are my friends,

they entice me

to the end.

They seduce me,

they are my friends.

I can't help but stay in the vicinity of their aroma.

The fresh smell of bark

encircles me in the dead of night.

Provocatively I dance in the dead of night,

there's no fright.

And when I awakened in that hospital bed,

my beloved trees were no more.

The sadness that one little fright brought to my life.

I rode around the hospital,

tired of lying in bed.

They pushed me to pediatrics.

I remembered once I used to play.

I played with an almond-colored doll.

Oh, how I loved that doll.

We would talk

and we would walk

through the hot park on sunny days.

We drank lemonade on the porch,

and watched the passersby.

When I looked through that ICU window,

I saw that rag doll.

Pale and petite,

helpless as can be,

but still full of life.

I want to murder the ghost who caused this pain.

Tie him to a tree and hang him like a slave.

Why did he have to hunt me

and make me burn that candle?

I want to murder that ghost that stole my home.

But for now I must wait for the unwrapping of these
    bandages from my body.

Then I will walk out these doors and prepare a
    casket for that apparition.

I can't wait to be uncovered, unmasked, and
    un-mummified

so I can finally seize that beast.

I know the ghost pushed that candle over while
    I slept so gently.

I know he tried to kill me.

He had warned me time and time again he would be
    the cause of my last breath.

As my husband walked through the hospital door,

all was revealed.

He is that beast.

Here he is, live and in the flesh,

the ghost that haunted my last few dreams.

Overwhelmed with hate, I tried to scream—

nothing came out.

I tried to move, but the bandages held me back.

I twisted and turned in an attempt to kick him.

I didn't move an inch.

He stepped toward me.

My heart palpitated.

I awakened.

It was only a dream.

A dream so mean

shouldn't be dreamed at all.

I rubbed my eyes and rolled over.

Beside me was that devilish,

full-of-malice ghost.

I took my pillow,

put it over his face.

I held it strongly,

with all my might.

This night will not end the same,

this night is in my hands.

A feeling of satisfaction fluttered through my body.

I took my candle that glimmered in the dark and threw

it on his breathless chest.

I striped down naked and ran to my trees.

I love my trees.

They are my friends,

they entice me,

they seduce me.

I love my trees.

We dance in praise,

observing the flames.

❧ CONDEMNATION

I know you,

you were there.

You were there when I said goodbye.

You were there when my house turned to ashes.

You were there as they lowered my husband's

    casket into the dirt.

You were there when my daughter took

    her last breath.

You called me a monster,

a crazy, insane woman who deserves to be

    locked away.

But you never once walked in my shoes.

You told the judge to put me to sleep.

But you never once laid your head where I laid mine.

Before you condemn me,

walk in my shoes.

Here's my story,

tape it to your ears,

feel my words,

let them penetrate your mind,

let them bounce off your thoughts.

Let them open up your soul.

Let them reveal my sorrow,

reveal my pain,

let them feed your inner being.

Let my words be your words.

Join with me,

mind,

body,

and soul.

East to west,

north to south,

Atlantic to Pacific,

become one with me.

Like the wind,

like the ocean,

one body,

one mind,

one soul.

But first you must not condemn,

you must feel my words,

let them connect to your soul,

let them connect to your mind like a leech,

grip your air like CO_2.

They must transform you,

mind,

body,

and soul.

Become one with me,

like a penis penetrating a vagina,

one body to another,

one soul to another,

feel my words as they penetrate your mind.

CAGED

Bear with my estranged mind,

I stare into space and try to put together the puzzle

of my thoughts.

I sit alone.

Pen and paper.

-I begin to write.

SLOPJAR

Piss out the piss,

shit out the shit,

simmer it,

in a slopjar.

Release all frustrations,

lay them to rest,

simmer them,

in a slopjar.

Simmer the lunatic thoughts,

the loneliness, the laughter, the lust,

the love,

the feelings of hurt and pain.

Simmer it all in a slopjar,

then throw it in the woods.

loneliness

A DOVE IN THE WIND

The darkest corners of my mind

shed tears on my pillow each night.

The dreary days of hatred

lie in these filthy corners,

buried in the pit of quietude that befalls my presence.

My every innocence taken away.

My youth buried six feet deep

    and vaulted in my mind.

The venom of a snake entangled in my very being,

it strangled my soul.

It stalked me by night and fed upon my fear.

This being,

this being I've never seen,

that destroyed my heart,

back then.

Back then,

when it was made of fragile glass,

and now it stands alone in my body,

hard,

solid,

stone.

And now I sit breathless,

unable to speak,

unable to move,

unable to stop his acts

of betrayal.

My tears run continuously.

My body lies lifeless,

broken like my heart,

beyond repair.

The flow of blood from

my veins,

to my arteries,

ceases to flow, the dream of life.

A new person is born,

the real me,

finally uncovered.

The old me put to death.

I become a dove in the wind.

I soar in the sky.

H-BOMB

Drowning in the pit of my suburban life,

wishing I could fly and leave this totalitarian

    life in the cage, to linger.

I would fly up to that dream I dreamed,

where dreams exploded into reality.

I would hold hands with the stars while chatting

    with the moon.

Opening up my soul, my mind, and even my legs

    to the orgasm of life.

H-bomb explosive power,

sparks erupting like a volcano.

I would burst into a million buds dangling on a vine.

There I would wait,

I would wait to ripen,

I would wait to bloom,

I would wait for the next orgasm life brings on.

Until then,

I dream,

I dream of holding hands with the stars,

I dream of chatting with the moon.

I dream and wait,

wait and dream,

for my day,

my special day,

when I will shine.

HAPPINESS AND PEACE

Once upon a time,

I traveled to the moon.

Once upon a time,

I sought a far-off place.

Once upon a time,

destruction stalked my path.

It hit so suddenly it slapped me in the face.

Once upon a time,

I did not know what to do.

I sought peace,

I sought happiness,

I sought until I found this place called Understanding.

Understanding was country, how I longed for the city.

The city was far, they called it Contentment.

My journey was long, so I packed my bags well.

Patience and Grace

filled my wallet with wealth.

Contentment was no better.

Oh, why did I go?

Where else shall I travel?

No one seemed to know,

so to the moon I went

to wish upon a star.

Happiness and Peace

are all I wish for.

Find me soon

so I can rest.

Find me soon

as I sit upon the moon.

PEACE, BE STILL

Too much drama stepping in my doorway,

too many whispers surrounding my presence.

Peace, be still.

I need a break,

let the words cease,

let the chatter die out.

Peace, be still.

This is not a soap opera.

The words cut slashes,

the whispers burn holes,

the chatter hangs feelings

and leaves you in disarray.

Peace, be still,

if just for a day.

ALL STAR SCENE

Cast down as an outcast,

I forecast misery

in the life I'm suppose to cast in.

But until the casket closes

I will endure,

I will endure never-ending suffering.

Until the casket closes,

I act out an all star scene.

JOYLESS

The careless hand that sliced my wrist

lingers in the depth of the night.

It plans to devour my soul and place me deep down.

I refuse to let it slaughter my life,

I refuse to let it steal my joy,

the joy that is left behind from all the years of

    sorrow and pain.

Oh wait,

wait a minute here,

I have no joy.

Go ahead, be that thief,

that thief that steals everyone's breath,

but I shall have the last laugh

because all you get from me is misery and pain.

Ha, ha, ha, ha.

Ha, ha, ha, ha,

Let my misery rot in your stomach,

let it tear at your brain like it tore at mine.

Take that knife and become like me,

a flaccid spoonful of dirt.

Lowered into the ground for no one to ever miss.

Be my guest and take your toll.

Accomplish your goal

but leave my soul.

As the drum rolls,

I sit and wait.

Take your toll

but leave my soul.

DADDY CURSED ME

I know this wouldn't have happened

    if daddy would have been there.

Where was daddy?

Not minding me.

Daddy cursed me.

I called for him every night;

only mommy answered.

I fell and pretended to be hurt;

only brother answered.

I hoped for him to hold me and bounce me

    on his knee;

only grandpa answered.

Where was daddy?

Not minding me.

He cursed me to this day,

not to trust, not to love, but to despise men.

I needed my daddy,

but he had no need for me.

I needed to be loved by the opposite sex,

but love was never there.

Many answered my call,

many scarred me,

none was daddy,

and daddy never knew

how much I needed his love.

I craved him,

praised him,

and he never came.

So here I am a fatherless bastard,

still without a daddy to call my own.

So here I am a fatherless bastard with nothing
    more to say.

✂ DREAM ACCOMPLISHED

The loneliness of tomorrow

burns at my soul.

The sorrow of today sits at my feet and mildews

    in my sight.

The festering smell of yesterday holds

    sorrowful memories.

How do we get through each day and move forward

    to a place of newness?

The pitiful stench of a willful soul gathers at my door.

I slam my door in despair.

There has to be more to living than sorrow and pain.

Where is the dream accomplished?

I lie in my bed breathing the air of yesterday's pain,

Where is the dream accomplished?

I spray perfume to cover the still smell

    of the day before,

it lingers

and lingers

in the darkness of the room.

Within seconds the true smell pierces,

it arrives on the surface, and there it sits,

it sits and stares.

It sits in my presence and crowds my body,

it suffocates my nostrils and leaves me

breathless,

breathless,

breathless.

My last breath slowly wiggles out into the mist

and drowns in the river of sorrow.

Where is the dream accomplished?

The breath of a sleepless night arrives in and exits out.

My feet out of bed never ever touch the floor.

For days I lie in bed.

Why?

Because I can.

I can lie here and be sad,

I can lie here and be in thought,

I can lie here and wish for death,

I can lie here because I can,

I can,

I can be in dismay,

I can be mad,

I can be sad,

but not for long.

❧ ANEW

The slumber of the day when the sun sets sail

romances me in the shadows of the evening.

I bathe in the rays that pierce my skin.

    I sauté in its touch.

I lie on my back and look up at the flourish of

    banana, berry-blue colors crossing the sky.

I wave the sun good night but only for a short while.

The bloodshed of the war,

when nights win the battle,

plays at my heart

until morning takes over.

The tar of the sky tears at my nerves,

it hides the demons that play in the fog,

it shelters the thieves that strike in the darkness,

it covers the sin that arrives with the stars.

And I rest my sleepless head till the sun rushes in and

    bring back the day

    that the demons once stole.

INTERLUDE

I sit in my cell with no hope at all. I sit in my cell hoping someone will call. For days I sit here and spill my heart to this pen and paper. Why did life have to be so cruel? And now I just sit here full of drugs, unaware of any drop of happiness or sanity. I just want to fly away to that place we are supposed to call home because here I do not belong. I did not mean to burn that house, I did not mean to say good bye. Maybe one day joy will come, but until it does, pen and paper, I will continue to write.

HELPLESS

My shattered heart can't ache any more.

I give up,

I throw in my towel,

I resign.

My pondering mind can't wonder any more.

I'm thoughtless,

I'm dumbfounded,

I'm free of freedom.

My broken bones can't move any more.

They're cracked,

they're weakened,

they're flaccid.

I lie here helpless

at the foot of your door.

Knock, knock

ENDLESS NIGHTS OF WATCHING

Endless nights of watching,

watching the passersby

passing by my dreams.

Dreams free of worry.

Endless nights of watching,

watching the slave bells churn,

churning to the rhythm,

the rhythm of the souls.

Endless nights of watching,

watching the African chants,

chanting to the rhythm,

the rhythm of the souls.

Nearly nude,

barely clothed,

dancing 'round a fire.

Endless nights,

endless nights of watching,

until the sun rises.

MELLOW, SWEET

Mellow, sweet remedies passing by my window,

a single tear runs down my cheek.

The fear of losing today to gain tomorrow

brings a shiver down my spine.

Another day gone,

another day older.

Mellow, sweet remedies,

tell me what to do.

A second tear runs down my cheek.

The fear of losing the sun to gain the moon

brings teardrops to my eyes.

Another night with morning to gain.

Mellow, sweet, mellow, sweet,

wipe my tears away.

Bind my fears of days to come and wash my body in

the temple of youth.

The temple of youth,

forever young.

Mellow, sweet remedies,

save my youth from days to come.

SANDY BEACHES

Sandy beaches,

glowing waters

describe my day in paradise.

The day I smiled for joy,

the day I forgot all pain,

the day the waters wrapped me in bliss.

Sandy beaches,

glowing water

describe my day in paradise.

All sin was forgiven,

all debts were paid,

all destruction was set aside.

Sandy beaches,

glowing water

describe the day my soul awakened

and my body was put to rest.

❧ THE PAST

I walked into a world of dragonflies and purple lilies,

upon a fern I set my glass,

I glided on the Mississippi

and walked a mile on the golden pavement

    of New Orleans.

I shook every hand that resembled temptation.

I lay on my back in the arms of sin

and looked up into a sky where I saw no tomorrow,

no future,

no hope,

no sign of help from my worldly folks.

The folks

I call home,

the folks who borrow,

the folks who lie,

who stole my heart and left it to rot.

That wasn't right,

not in my sight,

but here I am,

how about we toast.

Let's toast to the past.

Let's toast to the last.

Now that we're acquainted, you can kiss my ass.

WHO I AM

The star I thought I was

I lost in the sky.

The woman in the mirror

no longer fits my description.

I pop pill after pill,

hoping to find that place called home,

the place I belong,

the place where I am me,

but no such place seems to exist.

Only endless prescription pads and empty bottles fill my
presence.

Where did that star go?

I refuse to look any further.

I close my book,

I rest my case.

Tell me who I am.

I lie at night with sleepless thoughts and a strangled
mind.

I sit in the day with hopeless worries and bewildering

dreams which never cross at night.

I sleepwalk day by day with no hint of rest

or idea of shut eyes.

I just have to know this person

that stares back at me in the mirror,

this woman

with no place of happiness or belonging,

this woman

-I call me.

❧ SOUL SEARCHING

Judy Garland sang "Somewhere Over the Rainbow."

I've never ever seen a rainbow.

How do I search

for that unknown rainbow?

She sang over the rainbow.

What rainbow?

What rainbow?

I wish upon a star every night,

and I still wake up in sorrow.

I really want to see this place, over that rainbow,

where suffering is no more,

where peace will calm my sorrows.

I lay my head to sleep,

and, like always,

The pain overtakes my mind.

Tears pour down my face,

and that rainbow never appears.

So I just lie with my head on my pillow,

hoping that rainbow will appear

to take my sorrows away.

-Bear with my estranged mind,

pill after pill they feed my body.

I sit alone.

-Bear with my estranged mind,

I sit alone staring into space,

looking for that rainbow.

I try to put together the thoughts of my mind,

but they linger in pieces.

So I just sit alone in my chair staring out the window,

with my pen and paper.

I just write.

CANDLESTICKS AND ASHES

Wax just melted away upon my body,

drop by drop,

devouring my every spot.

The seconds were hours of torment.

The minutes, days of sadness and despair.

My body sweats with thirst,

my tongue drenched with dryness,

my thoughts,

no thoughts,

just a long itching of pain scattered in the breeze.

Candlesticks and ashes

lie beneath my feet.

The ashes of deceased beings and the candles that
    scorched them.

My dream is no more.

I awaken.

I must write.

I NEED A PENCIL

Most of these MFers don't write;

why are all these pencils so dull?

I guess that's Lucifer saying my story is not worth

dancing,

my words not worth ears.

My words aren't supposed to serenade

the ears of the people.

But

I see gold,

I see platinum,

I see diamond,

I see bank

because my message is yours,

my message is hers,

my message is words of wisdom.

My message inspires.

My message is owned by the thousands.

My message is heard by the millions.

My message is here!

Laughter

MOMMY ALWAYS SAID

Mommy always said

what I do in secret will bite me in the ass one day.

I never knew it would hurt so badly,

I never knew it would leave a hole,

I never knew how true it was.

Mommy always said

what I do in secret will bite me in the ass one day.

Never again will I tease that dog.

❧ GATORS

I remember as a child

the beautiful swamp at the edge of the river—

it rocked my world when the alligators gaped.

They wrestled and they swam and I watched

them in peace.

They didn't scare me.

They were my friends,

them darn alligators.

I loved them so.

As soon as I got grown,

I refused to leave their sight.

So now I take them everywhere I go,

from stores to parties they keep me company.

O, how I love my gators,

from my shoes to my purse, they bring style to my life.

THE SLOPPY MOPPY BAR

The story she told me started like this:

she awakened to a misty night,

gathered her things, and walked away.

Never to remember,

always to forget

what happened that night

in that dirty ole bar.

To this day that's the end of her story.

She gathered her things and walked away.

She never told me about the scars,

she never mentioned any of the bruises,

she only told me she gathered her things and walked
away.

The night was misty,

the smell was musty,

the moon was full, and the stars were scarce.

Other than that, I only know she gathered her things
and walked away.

Her clothes were torn,

her breath was still,

one shoe was missing,

and her hair astray.

And all she could describe was that misty night

and how she gathered her things and walked away.

So to this day

I still don't know,

I still wonder,

I still sit in sympathy,

for my pure ole friend

who never would tell me

what happened that night

at the Sloppy Moppy Bar.

❧ THE SLOPPY MOPPY 2

Sloppy Moppy,

with glass on the floors,

slippery hardwood wall to wall,

broken chairs,

and cracked lightbulbs.

Dark and gloomy but full of life.

The Sloppy Moppy, where many spend their pay.

The Sloppy Moppy is no place to play.

At the Sloppy Moppy they fight to the end

with all their might, they fight to win.

Breaking bottles and destroying chairs,

the Sloppy Moppy is no place to play.

Bottles cross the head,

chairs cross the back.

Truth be told,

the Sloppy Moppy is no place to be.

Try not to enter,

stay far,

far away

because the spirits are high and the music is sweet,

and someone's life is always at stake.

So take my advice

and make wise choices,

and stay far away

from the Sloppy Moppy Bar.

JOLLY MOLLY AT THE SLOPPY MOPPY

Jolly Molly ate her soup in her hospital bed.

Jolly Molly had a knot on her head.

She was bruised.

Her bones were broken.

She lay in bed with hair full of crabs.

She just stopped burning.

She just stopped crying.

It's such a shame because Jolly Molly was

always happy.

She always smiled.

She always sang.

Jolly Molly was always drunk.

Jolly Molly spent her days sleeping in peace on her

living room floor.

Every night she lived

in and out

of the Sloppy Moppy bar.

Drink after drink, vodka, rum, tequila, or gin,

she drowned herself in cup after cup.

Last night was no different,

at the Sloppy Moppy Bar.

Jolly Molly lay pissy drunk across a pool table.

It isn't a secret,

the men were eager,

and they all took their turn with ole Jolly Molly.

Until a wife walked in, filled with anger,

and there went the bottles,

chairs,

and fists,

flying through the air

at the Sloppy Moppy Bar.

This is why

penicillin,

bandages,

a razor and cream

were all Miss Molly needed

    when she exited the hospital doors.

JOHNNY WHOREMAN

Stop the details!

I don't give a shit!

You lied!

I don't care!

Stop the bullshit!

Give my mind some peace and rest!

Leave the lies

to the flies!

I don't care how you broke your arm!

I don't care how bad it hurts!

Leave me alone!

I don't give a damn!

So you broke your arm!

Don't you think you deserved it?

Rolling around in that whore's bed!

Whores are not free,

they charge fares.

Not once did you think her pimp would come!

Where was your money,

you rotten ole fool?

Leave me alone! I don't give a damn!

Go back to your whore,

and leave me to rest.

SLOPPY MOPPY 3

Terror constantly strikes in the musty,

still Sloppy Moppy Bar.

Morning,

noon,

or night,

expect a fight.

The Sloppy Moppy,

where Satan resides.

He takes his pick,

each soul condemned,

each life forsaken.

The Sloppy Moppy is the demons' playpen.

They sit in gin,

covered with sin.

Expect the worst

because some leave in a hearse.

❧ PRECIOUS PEACHES

Precious Peaches,

big and round.

Precious she was,

with her beautiful smile.

You could see her,

from a mile.

Poor,

Precious Peaches,

big and round.

But precious she was,

sweet as can be,

juicy,

-oh yeah,

with her plump belly.

Precious Peaches was my best friend.

Each time I looked in the mirror,

she gave me a wink.

Precious Peaches was my mirror image.

lust

❧ A NIGHT OF LOVE

Screaming red diamonds,

set sail thought my veins,

coasting down my spine,

entering an erotic zone.

My lover navigates the search for my sweet spots,

his fingertips arouse my inner soul.

I knew this love wouldn't last long,

I knew his love was only short-lived.

The moonlight glow taunted my eyes.

The darkness of his car relaxed my joints.

I knew this night's love would be short-lived,

so I just lay in lust to experience his love,

if only for one night.

✿ TAKE MY FLOWER

Fresh lavender, waken my senses.

Blissful eucalyptus, serenade my soul.

Pussy willow splendor, caress my body.

Roses, prey on my heart's desire.

Let the romance dance in the breeze.

Smell my sweet nectar.

Bond with my petals.

Let my pistils sway in the wind as they

hypnotize your entire being.

Take my flower,

let it melt in your grasp.

Like sugar on your tongue,

honey on your lips,

devour the sweet nectar.

Blissful eucalyptus, stir up his soul.

❧ STAND STILL IN THE WIND

Stand still in the wind.

Feel my breeze between your legs.

Feel my breath warm your body.

Stand still in the wind.

STILL STANDING IN THE WIND

Still standing in the wind,

let me caress your being,

let me ease your pain.

Feel my desire,

feel my passion,

feel my hand between your thighs.

Feel the sensation.

Are you still there?

Still standing in the wind,

waiting for my seductive touch,

my sensual caress,

my mind-binding kiss?

This one is for you,

for your pleasure,

for your desire.

Don't be scared to feel the breeze tiptoe in.

Stand still in the wind

while I light your candle.

Wind, be easy.

Let me set a flame.

Let the oceans wave,

let the boats set sail,

let the pastures flow,

let the flowers dance.

Keep still in the wind. This one is for you.

Keep still in the wind while everything moves.

✌ TOLL

I need your love,

I need your affection,

I need you to hold my hand when all hope is gone.

I need your smile to brighten up my day.

I need your assurance when my life is in disarray.

Before you walk out that door,

remember you are the one.

You are the one who brightens my day,

you are the one who possesses the key.

You got the key to my heart.

Before you walk out that door,

remember,

wait, hold up,

I lost my train of thought.

Hold up,

I remember.

Now I remember.

You are the one who hurt my feelings.

You are the one who

told me I wasn't shit,

that my life amounted to a pile of manure.

You are the one who deserves to leave,

you deserve to suffer a lover's wage.

So close the chapter,

turn the page.

You will never hear my voice again,

so bye bye.

Our love has paid its toll.

✂ THE ONES I LOVE

The ones I love,

I always lose.

The special ones that trap my heart and steal my
    breathe away.

But in my mind they still linger.

Even after

the moment's lost,

I still can remember.

The ones I want,

the ones I crave,

the ones that linger in my mind,

I never seem to keep.

I lose them by choice,

I lose them by reason,

I lose them because I can't seem to find that perfect one
    to fill his shoes.

Whose shoes?

His shoes,

my perfect mate's shoes.

My perfect mate I fantasize about—

his shoes are hard to fill.

My dreams of him are hard to replace,

so until the day fate whispers his name in my ear,

I will wander this world with love for him.

Love that will never part,

love that drenches my body,

shines through my soul,

and brings this miraculous glow to the surface

    of my face.

Until fate whispers in my ear,

"He's the one,

he's the one,

he's the one to fill these shoes,

he's the one who lingered in your dreams."

I will love him

until I find him.

I will love him

until I can love no more.

❁ IT'S REAL

Outstanding,

brilliant,

and intriguing words

pressed against my heart

when his words rolled into my ear.

Smooth,

charming,

romantic words

slipped into the pores of my body.

It was real,

his touch,

his words.

It was real,

it all belonged to me.

So I thought,

so I thought,

and I was wrong.

The words were lifeless,

senseless,

meaningless words of crap

that had filled my spirit with bliss.

I was wrong,

they were right,

right when they said he was a disgrace,

right when they said his love wasn't true.

Meaningless words of crap

pumped into my heart like waves from a defibrillator.

Time I wasted wrapped in his bliss,

bewitched by his smell.

His meaningless words of crap were nothing

but breath in the air.

And now I breathe,

I breathe the fresh air of a new day.

My heartache,

my pain,

my sadness is uplifted,

and now I breathe

a joyous breeze of Mississippi air.

And now

I am free,

free to be,

free to be a mangy dog.

❧ MISUSED

The wicked ole man slid into my life.

He stole my heart ten times over.

He came undetected,

bearing many gifts,

gifts that stole my heart and locked it in a box.

I was swept off my feet by his charming eyes;

    his mean look

sent shivers over my body.

I had plans for him.

Plans to make him mine.

Plans to make him smile.

But all the while I was just a rock in his path,

a paper towel to be trashed.

I was just a body with no mind,

a thing,

an animal,

a woman, a woman,

a woman men despise,

a woman

men misused,

a woman

set aside.

For days I cried for him,

for weeks I watched his picture,

but in the end

I knew

he was missing out

because I am a woman,

a gift from GOD almighty.

❧ MY SISTER

Reach into the endless pit

and tell me what lies beneath,

beneath the hidden thoughts and sleepless nights.

Tell me the secrets you hold so dear,

the mysteries of your life

tucked away for no one to see.

The hidden secrets of love.

The love that blackened your eye.

The love that made you cry yourself to sleep.

Love sometimes hurts,

and your pain is real,

buried within your soul too deep to be released.

But I am here,

not to judge,

but to open up the door.

I can tell you the secret to where true happiness lies.

High up in the clouds

is where I found my love.

He was so addictive and seductive,

he took away my pain and he can take away yours.

Remember happiness is in the sky.

Stretch your heart to the sky and lie in his arms,

taste his sweetness,

let the honey cover you

until you are free.

Swim in his nectar,

get high on his drug,

behold the big beautiful blue sky and feel its warmth.

And just as the sky is blue,

and your tears are true

and run down your cheeks

and seep through my pores when I wipe them away,

pain is not forever.

So remember joy soon to be,

so enter into the sky

and let GOD lead your life.

Tell the demons no more.

Walk through the fog and scattered dreams.

It's over now,

the past is no more.

❦ POOR OLE YOU

Just because I asked to be the apple of your eye,

you belittled me,

you cursed me.

Your ass you gave,

your ass I kissed.

How could you belittle the apple of your eye?

I am the object of near perfection,

the princess of peace,

the goddess of the earth.

The soul of an angel I possess.

How could you?

How could you?

How could you abuse me?

Just because I asked to be the apple of your eye.

Look here now,

look here now,

I am now the splinter in your finger,

the mountain on your back,

the itch you just can't reach.

Let me be more exact:

I am that bitch!

I am that bitch who pierces your soul.

I am that bitch who grips your mind.

Sleep you want, but sleep you shall not get.

Rest you will never see.

Rest?

Who, you?

No,

Not ever,

Your peace is destroyed.

Poor ole you,

Poor ole you,

Poor ole you.

I just wanted to be the apple of your eye.

🌹 LOVE SWEET LOVE

Love, sweet love,

how I wish you were near.

I dream upon the day

you take my hand to wed.

Love, sweet love,

Dirty my body with pleasure,

fill me with your love,

caress me with your words.

Whisper in my ear

lustful melodies that spiral sensation.

Love, sweet love,

make love to my body.

Show me ecstasy because love is not enough.

Love, sweet love,

shelter me for the night.

lucifer

DEMON ON MY SOUL

Overwhelmed with despair that dangles over my head

like those things in cradles,

who knows what they are called,

wait,

they are called mobiles,

see i'm overwhelmed:

like there's a monkey on my back,

a demon on my soul

creating this monster bucking inside me,

ready to come out

and set foot in this world.

My mind has contractions.

The baby is ready to be born.

I scream

and I scream,

and the contractions keep coming.

My pupils dilate,

my legs wide open, but out my mouth comes

a drunken sailor,

out my bones comes a demon's arms, and I kill

and I kill

and I strangle any nuisance.

I rip out veins and crush arteries.

My baby is born,

and I am put to rest.

His name is Lucifer, just like his daddy.

His words like fire:

when he speaks,

you burn.

When he crawls,

he slithers.

He's my child,

ready to spit fire,

ready to unleash his rage.

His name is Lucifer, just like his father.

Call me crazy,

call me insane,

little will I hear

because my ears sit covered,

covered in bullshit,

six feet of it,

all stacked upon my body,

and now my baby lives.

I'm sorry you missed me,

but for him to live,

I had to die.

Only one body,

one mind,

and two souls,

his and mine,

and mine was bruised,

fragile,

and weak.

So I just retired in peace for him to take over.

Sorry you missed me.

You came too late.

Talk to my baby.

Try to change his fate.

❧ PUT TO REST

He's knocking at the door, and I refuse to answer his
    persistent knock.

He's ringing my phone, and I refuse to answer his
    persistent ring.

He has arrived already, but I am not yet ready:

my hair not done,

my clothes not on,

my smell not fresh

'cause I've been lying here.

For days my body has not moved

in this ditch,

my soul put to rest,

and now he knocks

on my casket door.

My soul is put to rest.

THE TERROR OF NIGHT

Look,

did you see that?

That terror that came out of nowhere?

That same terror awakens me in a midnight's sleep.

It's the terror of night,

it always rushes up on me.

At any time,

it can fright.

I turn on all my lights and pace the floor.

I close my curtains, then peep up at the moon.

The moon smiles back,

it sees my fears.

I think it teases me

because it winks its eye.

It hates me

because it knows I hate it,

I despise it,

the terror of night.

I feel like a victim,

and it comes every night to steal my light.

It handcuffs me to terror

and locks me in fright.

The terror of night

creeps thought the windows and darkens my rooms.

It strikes my heart and squeezes it like a lemon,

it squeezes the juice out of my flaccid body.

I fall to death,

but only for a short while.

✂ TWISTED

They say I have a twisted mind,

but whose mind hasn't been twisted

by all the shit the world has dumped

and baked into an apple pie?

Yes,

my mind is twisted!

No,

I don't care who knows!

The end!

Sorry,

I can't just end it like that.

The beginning,

the beginning of a new era,

the beginning of my twisted mind,

the beginning of a whole new breed.

So,

my mind is sick!

It's sick from all the annoying people

getting on my damn nerves

morning,

noon,

and night.

Peace I never receive.

"Leave me alone!"

I scream,

"Leave me alone!"

They look at me

and continue to talk

about the weather,

about the news,

about the way their feet hurt when they stand,

about all the bullshit

I don't give a damn about.

"Leave me alone!"

I scream out loud.

More chatter,

more chatter,

it never ceases or decreases.

Only sleep brings peace,

so now I am going to lie down

and give my twisted mind some rest.

lord

PRAYER FOR FORGIVENESS

My heart cries out a million cries of pain.

My soul is not at rest.

I'm torn by indecisive thoughts.

I'm not at ease,

I respond with rage because of the aggression hidden
deep within my soul,

but my love is genuine.

It surpasses the sky and stretches past the oceans.

Overlook my malice and see the real me,
who means no harm.

Forgive my sins and never stop loving me.

Amen.

❧ SINFUL SOUL

Let sin be your teacher,

it will never lead you wrong.

Let sin be your savior,

it reveals all transgressions.

It shows you your strength.

It shows you your guilt.

You know you want forgiveness.

In your eyes I see

your pain,

your suffering,

your doubt,

your lies,

your feelings of hopelessness.

They stir self-pity in your being.

You can't hide it with spirits,

with smokes,

with needles,

or pills.

Just let sin be your teacher,

it's the only way out.

Reveal your sin and let GOD in.

No other key will open the lock.

Just let sin be your teacher

and let GOD in.

❧ TO ALL WHO WANT TO KNOW

The rage of a black man hung from a tree

    lies within my heart.

The rope,

the dangling limbs represented my past.

It gathered in my mind and stomped on my cerebellum.

It took my breath away when I reached for happiness.

It crowded my dreams and ruptured my thoughts.

It owned my soul.

The rope suffocated me at night and loosened in the

    mornings.

The limbs shook up and down when I was happy and

    stiffened when I was weak.

It haunted my mind.

The railroad tracks my ancestors laid were the path of

    my journey.

To and fro I wandered the world, wondering what my

    purpose was.

Now I know.

I hang from my tree, and like my ancestors I give my

life for what I believe in

and for Him in whom I trust.

The truth has been revealed!

I keep the word of GOD strapped to my chest

    like a bulletproof vest

protecting me,

guiding me,

and sheltering me.

No weapon will prosper against me.

My love for Him buries my rage,

his love for me buries my sins.

He has released the rope

I once hung from.

My heart burst into a thousand pieces, scattering

    throughout the world like pollen,

hoping to fall on fertile ground.

Now I know,

his Word goes forth in the ears of the unborn and,

    upon birth, the offspring springs forth healthy,

pure, and a believer

of the Word and its purpose:

to scatter the thoughts coming against the

    Word of GOD.

Let it be known:

He is alive

for all to take hold of what He has to say.

Buried within your soul lies the key to eternal life.

Open the gate and let Him in.

To all who want to know,

He is real.

SEARCH FOR JOY

The wonders of pain never seem to end.

I never have to wonder because they never leave my
bones.

The wonders of joy linger in the corners of the dark
alleys of my mind

and never seem to find their way to the light.

I wish to plan the great escape

where I will loosen my shackles and wander out of the
dark alleys,

where I will find my joy,

joy in seeking righteousness,

joy in seeking GOD,

joy in living,

joy in the great escape away from my
corruption and misery,

joy in finding peace,

peace within myself,

peace within GOD,

peace to spread to the entire world

by walking into the light.

✿ SELF-WORTH

For what I want to know is a mystery in the dark.

I seek to find out the truth of my self-worth.

My body may be whole,

my mind may be lucid,

my being a breath in the air, but still I seek to find my
self-worth.

Why was I put here to suffer in the distresses put on me
by the world?

But your ole wretched soul is a pebble in the world's
eyes and spit in the face of the most high, yet you
still sit in joy.

Why are you rich and I poor when I was the one who
stayed pure of sin?

What is my self-worth in this world?

You own mansions,

I own the shirt on my back, so what is my self-worth?

We both stand here in the presence of GOD,

and I am only a drunk who indulges in his Word.

I wash away misery with the Word of GOD,

I overdose on it.

It fills my throat in the hour of the night when my
mouth dries from the burning of my soul's
mourning.

What is my self-worth?

I am a glutton.

I feed on the Word evening and morning.

Breakfast, lunch, and dinner, it fills my stomach.

When I am in starvation, when the world refuses to
feed me love, what is my self-worth?

I'll tell you.

My self-worth is greater than anything that has ap-
peared on earth,

my self-worth is intensified with greatness,

my self-worth is of GOD,

my self-worth is self-sustaining,

my self-worth is irresistible,

my self-worth is outstanding,

my self-worth is of GOD,

my self-worth has taken me to heaven in my final hour.

My self-worth is all I have because without my self-
worth I am nothing.

Remember your self-worth because without it

the world turns you upside-down and stomps on your
heart.

Without self-worth you become nothing but a puppet
to be toyed with,

a soul to be engulfed.

Everyone has self-worth, just tap into the self-worth
GOD put here for you to indulge in.

✂ WRITTEN WORDS

Here I am again,

writing my heart out for the Lord,

bruising my hands from typing,

screaming my mind into the world

by using soundless,

 powerful

interpretations of what seem to be words.

But not spoken words,

because spoken words are never heard,

but written words,

my written words,

sent down from above and placed upon your table for

    all to eat of.

My written words

will tear at your brain and cause convulsions.

Ordained by GOD almighty

to spread truth to the unknowing,

faith to the young,

and wisdom from living.

These are my written words.

✖ PRAISE GOD

A famous writer once said,

"Fame is only a step away from GOD,

a step backwards into the bottomless pit,

where the snakes wait to devour your soul.

Fame is only the devil's den

that we all wish to lie in."

But when she made these statements,

she was drugged,

she was drunk,

she herself laid face-down in the devil's blood,

full from tasting all his wine.

She herself was scarred because his name was tattooed

across her forehead.

She made that statement,

then sat upon his lap.

She wobbled in his nest and smoked up all his

thoughts.

She chatted with the demons and soaked up

all their rage.

And when the devil came to see them,
they were all praising GOD.

✿ PRAISE GOD 2

My sin has paid its toll,

the devil will soon collect.

Soon he will come to gather and take his tokens home.

Swiftly through the air,

he wastes no time on pace.

I guess I will just sit and pray

since my sins are plenty.

 When he arrived,

he arrived quite quickly,

quietly he came,

but to my surprise,

when the devil arrived to take his toll,

an angel stopped him in the midst.

Gabriel blew his trumpet

and Jesus' blood came dripping down.

Redemption had taken its course,

 and the angels begin to sing.

Praise GOD,

Praise GOD,

were the only words you could hear.

The praises rose to the rooftops

and echoed in the countryside.

All could hear the shouts of salvation,

and all could hear the jittering of bones

coming from the demons shaking.

 Scared with dismay,

they had nowhere to go

but to the bottomless pit,

where forever they will fall

and never reach joy.

So now that my time has come,

worries I have no more,

for salvation took its course,

and rescued me from the pit of Hell,

and now I must praise,

praise GOD for my salvation.

I DREAM

Come round my way, into my world,

    and see my dreams:

I hurt,

I feel,

I need.

I dream evil thoughts of furious shadows of blood

    paved across my chest.

I hurt like you,

I feel like you,

I need like you,

I dream like you.

I dream oceans of sadness and puddles of rejoicing.

I dream life, and in life there's death.

I hurt from life,

I hurt from living,

I hurt because my back holds a thousand scars

    of withered dreams and

people drowned by lakes of evilness,

lakes of blood,

lakes of my loved ones and your loved ones who have

passed, and our lives which are passing.

I dream to open up and swallow my sadness and pain.

I dream of demons overtaking my soul and

Jesus coming to my rescue.

I dream of streets paved with gold.

I dream of life.

I dream of the ending which is the beginning.

The beginning of thought and enlightenment:

no more pain,

no more suffering,

no more locks,

no more wars.

A brand-new you,

a brand-new me.

I dream because I cry.

I cry to God to clear the world,

I cry to the angels to feel my pain.

I cry to you to feel the same.

My tears knock at Jesus' door.

My pain enters his bones.

He cuddles me in his arms and tells me no
more worries.

I wake up wrapped in a blanket of love and
overflowing grace.

No more hurt,

no more need,

no more pain.

SORROW

Who knew my heart would ache like this,

who knew the pain I carried,

beaten on my back by whips of steel.

I lie broken, crushed, dismembered by the lies

    of betrayal.

Lord, help me now,

I'm a bruised woman

tortured by withered dreams and faulty words.

I sit amongst demons and bitter souls.

I'm a bruised woman

beaten down by false love,

false hope,

false words.

I sit alone clouded by satan's heroes.

I suffocate on their stench,

I vomit from their touch.

Lord, help me now,

I'm amongst the dead.

Awaken me like Lazarus.

Anoint my head with oil.

Breathe life into my lungs and grace upon my soul.

Make me a cleansed woman,

cleansed of aches and pain,

sorrow and shame.

Erase the devil's curse

and write me a lullaby.

Let me soar,

let me fly let me enter

eternal happiness.

I now sit a cleansed woman.

GOODBYE

Until the end I smile.

My greatness illuminates the sky.

Until the end I pray.

My greatness comes from prayer.

Until the end I say goodbye,

goodbye to all from the past.

Until the end,

until the end,

when we shall meet once again.

Author's Biography

Ingrid Jennings, a Louisiana native, graduated from Palm Beach Atlantic University with a bachelor's of science in biology and a minor in chemistry. She later attended Nova Southeastern University where she received a master's of science in reading education. Her hobbies include reading, writing, and driving fast on I-95.

Ingrid Jennings now resides in West Palm Beach, Florida with her husband and son. She can be reached at: ingridjennings.com

P.O. Box 223204
West Palm Beach, FL 33422

CPSIA information can be obtained at www.ICGtesting.com
Printed in the USA
LVOW080400110812

293815LV00003B/5/P